PAUL'S SHIPWRECK

Activity Book for Beginners

Bible Pathway
— Adventures® —

Paul's Shipwreck Activity Book for Beginners

Bible Pathway Adventures® is a trademark of BPA Publishing Ltd.
Defenders of the Faith® is a trademark of BPA Publishing Ltd.

ISBN: 978-1-7771601-8-0

Author: Pip Reid
Creative Director: Curtis Reid

For free Bible resources including coloring pages, worksheets, puzzles and more, visit our website at:

www.biblepathwayadventures.com

 # Introduction for Parents

Enjoy teaching your children about the Bible with our *Paul's Shipwreck Activity Book for Beginners*. Packed with lesson plans, worksheets, coloring pages, and puzzles to help educators just like you teach children a Biblical faith. Includes scripture references for easy Bible verse look-up and a handy answer key for teachers.

Bible Pathway Adventures helps educators teach children a Biblical faith in a fun and creative way. We do this via our Activity Books and free printable activities – available on our website: www.biblepathwayadventures.com

Thanks for buying this Activity Book and supporting our ministry. Every book purchased helps us continue our work providing free Classroom Packs and discipleship resources to families and missions around the world.

The search for Truth is more fun than Tradition!

★BONUS★

Our illustrated Shipwrecked! storybook is available for download.
Type the link into your browser to get your FREE copy today!
https://BookHip.com/RKVZDT

Table of Contents

LESSON 1 | Lesson Plan
Paul sails to Rome

Teacher: _____

Today's Bible passages: Acts 25:6-12 and Acts 27:1-4

Welcome prayer:
Pray a simple prayer with the children before you begin the lesson.

Lesson objectives:
In this lesson, children will learn:
1. Where the Roman Emperor lived
2. Who took Paul to Italy by boat

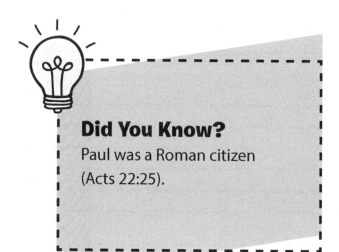

Did You Know?
Paul was a Roman citizen (Acts 22:25).

Bible lesson overview:
Many years ago there lived a man named Paul. He told people that Yeshua (Jesus) was the Messiah. But some people did not want Paul to talk about the Messiah. They made a plan to kill him. The Roman rulers heard about the plan. They rescued Paul and put him in prison in a city called Caesarea. "I have done nothing wrong," said Paul. "I want the Roman emperor to decide my case." The Romans agreed to send Paul to Rome to meet the emperor. This is the city where the Roman emperor lived. A soldier named Julius was told to take Paul to Rome by ship. Julius was kind to Paul. He let his friends take care of him along the way.

Let's Review:

Questions to ask your students:

1. Why did the religious leaders want to kill Paul?
2. Who rescued Paul?
3. Who did Paul want to meet in Rome?
4. Who was told to take Paul to Italy?
5. How did Paul travel to Rome?

 A memory verse to help children remember God's Word:

"It was decided to sail to Italy." (Acts 27:1)

Activities:

Connect the dots: Paul the apostle
Worksheet: What did Paul eat in prison?
Bible craft: Paul in prison
Worksheet: Trace the Words
Worksheet: P is for Paul
Let's learn Hebrew: Sha'ul
Coloring page: To Caesar you shall go!
Worksheet: What is heavy?
Worksheet: Sailing away…
Worksheet: Paul sails to Rome
Worksheet: The Roman Emperor
Worksheet: Tzitzits

 Closing prayer:

End the lesson with a small prayer.

Paul the apostle

The Romans kept Paul in prison (Acts 24:27).
Connect the dots to see the picture of Paul.

Paul's breakfast

What do you think Paul ate for breakfast in prison?
Draw Paul's breakfast. Use your imagination!

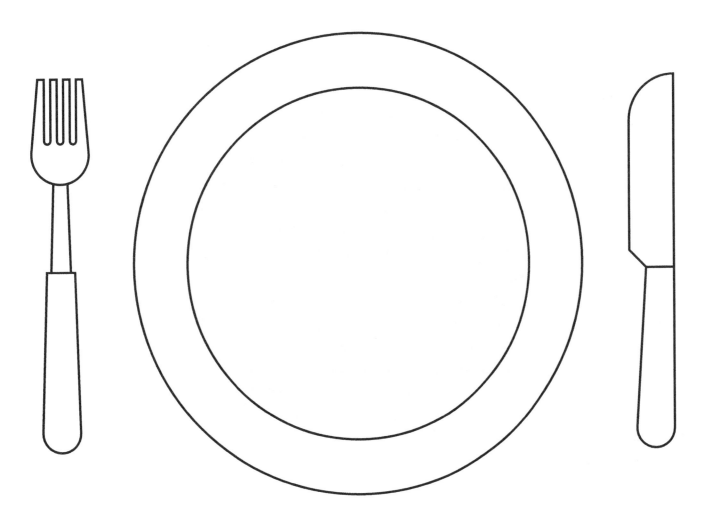

🌿 Trace the Words 🌿

Color the pictures.

Paul

ship

bible

Rome

10

P is for Paul

Paul taught people about the Messiah (Acts 26:23).
Trace the words. Color the picture.

P is for Paul

✹ Sha'ul ✹

Paul was a Hebrew from the tribe of Benjamin,
one of the twelve tribes of Israel (Philippians 3:5).
His Hebrew name was Sha'ul and his Greek name was Paul.

Sha'ul

שָׁאוּל

Paul

 Let's write!

Practice writing Paul's Hebrew name on the lines below.

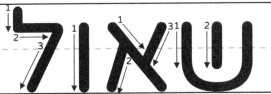

שָׁאוּל

Try this on your own.
Remember that Hebrew is read from RIGHT to LEFT.

"To Caesar you shall go!"

(Acts 25:12)

What is heavy?

A ship is big and heavy.
Circle and color the heavy things.

🌿 Sailing away... 🌿

Paul sailed to Rome on a ship. Trace the word Rome.
Color the pictures that start with the letter r.

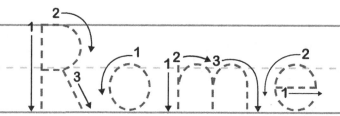

dress

raft

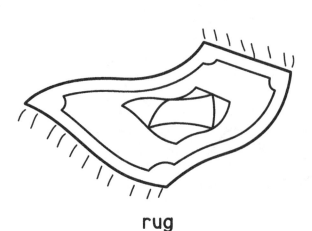

rug

rocket

Paul sails to Rome

Imagine you are Paul. What items would you take with you to Rome? Choose four items and draw them in the suitcase.

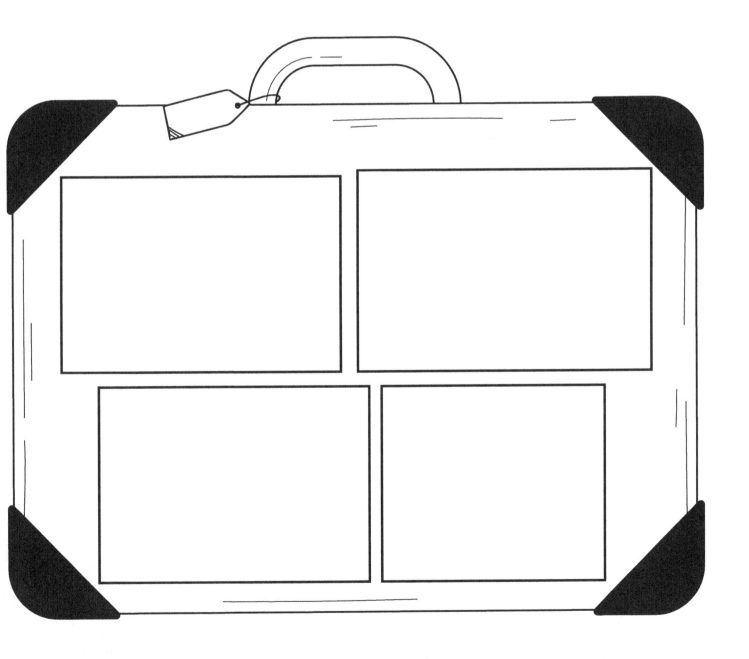

The Roman Emperor

The leader of the Roman empire was called an emperor. Paul wanted to meet him in Rome (Acts 25:11). Color the pictures of a Roman emperor, and then draw your own picture of an emperor.

Tzitzits

Paul was an Israelite from the tribe of Benjamin, one of the twelve tribes of Israel (Romans 11:1). God told the Israelites to wear tassels on their clothes (Numbers 15:38). This helped them remember the commandments. These tassels are called tzitzits.

Color and trace the set of tzitzits below.

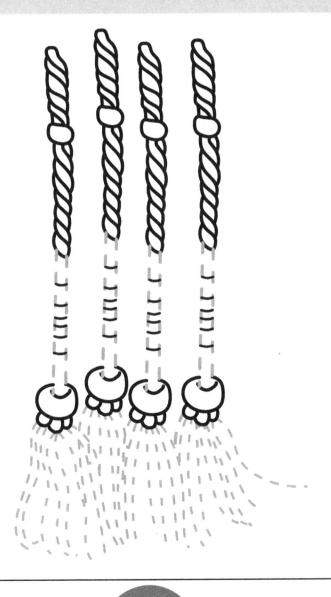

LESSON 2

Lesson Plan
Paul's warning

Teacher: _____

Today's Bible passage: Acts 27:7-15

Welcome prayer:
Pray a simple prayer with the children before you begin the lesson.

Lesson objectives:
In this lesson, children will learn:
1. The Hebrew name for Day of Atonement
2. Why Paul wanted to stay in Fair Havens

Did You Know?
Yom Kippur is also known as the Day of Atonement. This was the only time of the year the High Priest entered the Holy of Holies.

Bible lesson overview:
Paul and Julius sailed to Myra. There Julius found another ship sailing to Italy. The men boarded the ship and sailed across the sea. Soon, a strong wind began to blow and they sailed slowly for many days. The ship finally stopped in the port of Fair Havens. God's Feast of Yom Kippur (Day of Atonement) was over and winter was coming. It was dangerous to sail a ship across the sea during the winter months. "If we sail the ship, there will be a lot of trouble on this trip. The ship may be lost!" But the captain did not listen to Paul. He set sail to another city. On the way, the wind blew harder and harder and took the ship away. The captain could not sail his ship!

Let's Review:
Questions to ask your students:
1. Why was it hard to sail the boat?
2. What did Paul say to the captain?
3. Did the captain listen to Paul?
4. Why did the captain want to sail to Phoenix?
5. What have you learned about Paul so far?

 A memory verse to help children remember God's Word:
"We sailed slowly for many days." (Acts 27:7)

Activities:
Worksheet: I spy!
Worksheet: W is for water
Worksheet: S is for storm
Connect the dots: A Roman helmet
Coloring page: The Sabbath
Banner worksheet: Tribe of Benjamin
Map activity: Island of Crete
Bible activity: Paul sails to Rome
Bible word search puzzle: Paul sails to Rome
Worksheet: In winter I wear…
Worksheet: My compass
Worksheet: Matching pairs
Worksheet: Let's draw

 Closing prayer:
End the lesson with a small prayer.

🌿 I spy! 🌿

It was dangerous to sail a boat during winter. The weather was bad. Color the same object a single color. Then count each type of object and write the number on the label.

★ W is for water ★

is for
water

S is for Storm

The ship sailed into a storm (Acts 27:15).
Trace the letters. Color the picture.

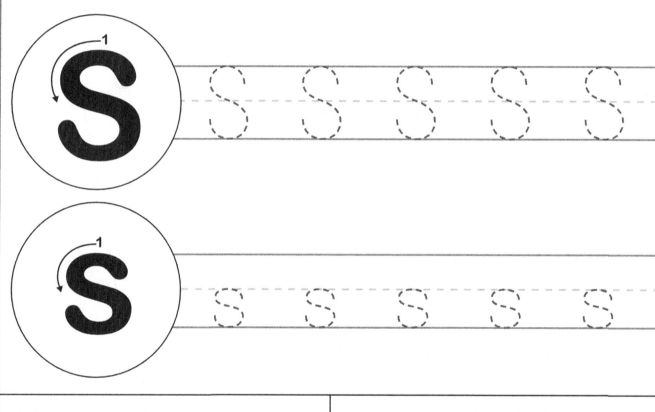

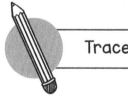
Trace the letter s

Color the stormy waves

storm

Try writing these letters on your own.

❧ Connect the dots ❧

Julius was a Roman soldier (Acts 27:1). He wore a helmet.
Connect the dots to show the helmet.

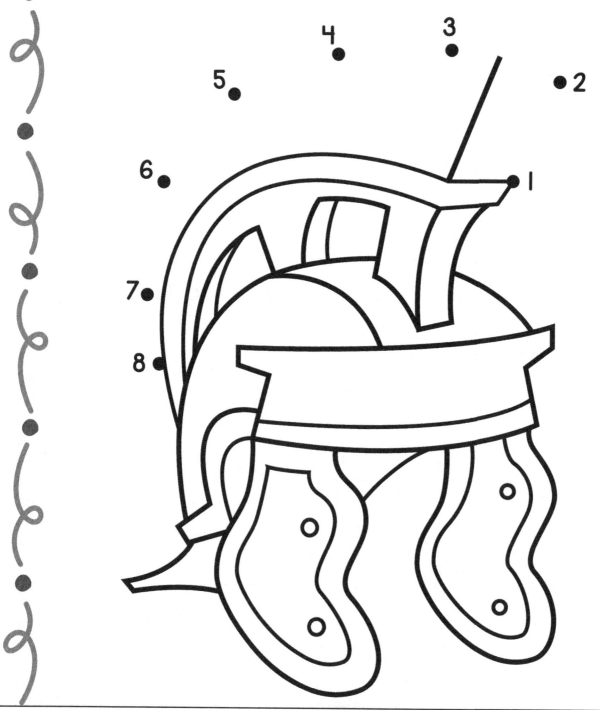

🌿 The Sabbath 🌿

Yom Kippur is a Sabbath (Leviticus 23).
The Sabbath is a day of rest for God's people.

Remember the Sabbath Keep it Holy

Tribe of Benjamin

Paul was an Israelite from the tribe of Benjamin (Romans 11:1). The tribe of Benjamin is one of the twelve tribes of Israel. Color the banner.

BENJAMIN

Island of Crete

The ship captain wanted to sail from Fair Havens to Phoenix (Acts 27). Did they make it? Draw a line from Fair Havens to Phoenix. Color the map.

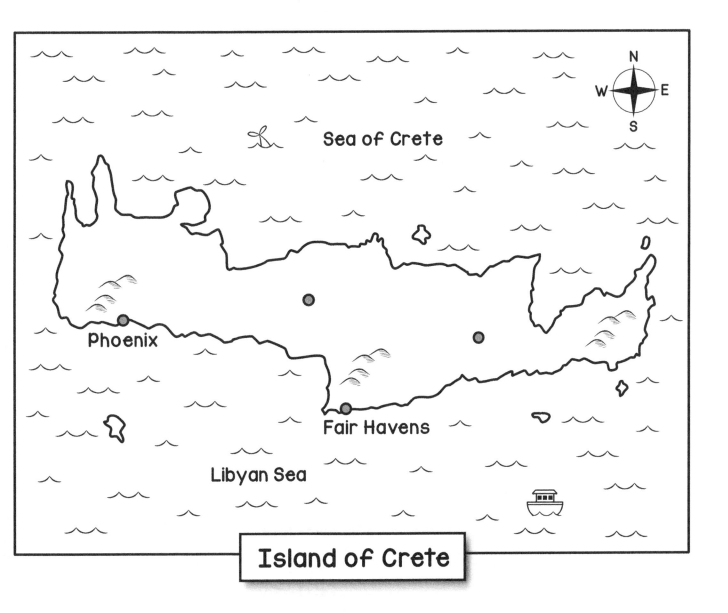

Island of Crete

Paul sails to Rome

Find and circle each of the words from the list below.

G	L	F	C	S	P
Y	O	V	V	H	A
B	R	D	C	I	U
S	A	I	L	P	L
W	I	N	D	U	W
S	T	O	R	M	E

GOD   PAUL
SHIP   WIND
STORM   SAIL

🌿 In winter I wear... 🌿

Winter is cold and stormy.
No wonder Paul didn't want to sail to Rome!
Color the clothes blue that you wear in the wintertime.

coat

hat

jacket

scarf

dress

t-shirt

singlet

🌿 Matching pairs 🌿

Draw a line between the matching objects.
Color the matching objects the same way.

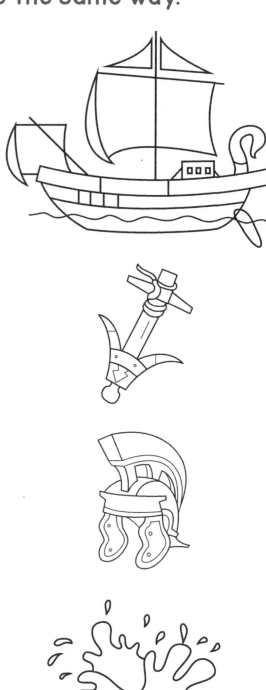

The Ship

Paul sailed to Rome on a ship (Acts 27:1).
Draw a picture of the ship.

LESSON 3 | Lesson Plan
The storm

Teacher: _____

Today's Bible passage: Acts 27:18-26

Welcome prayer:
Pray a simple prayer with the children before you begin the lesson.

Lesson objectives:
In this lesson, children will learn:
1. How the men tried to save the ship
2. God's promise to everyone on the ship

Did You Know?
The only Bible that people had at the time of Paul the apostle was the Old Testament.

Bible lesson overview:
The wind blew very hard and the waves grew higher and higher. The men tried to save the boat by throwing the cargo into the water. But the storm did not stop and the men were scared they would die. For many days they did not see the sun or stars. Then Paul stood up and said, "Men, do not worry. The angel of God told me that everyone on this boat will not die. God has promised to save you. But we will crash into an island."

Let's Review:

Questions to ask your students:

1. What did the men do to try and save the boat?
2. Why did the men think they were going to die?
3. What message did the angel of God give Paul?
4. What did the men not see for a long time?
5. Do you think Paul was scared of the storm?

 A memory verse to help children remember God's Word:

"God will save your lives." (Acts 27:24)

Activities:

Coloring page: Julius
Worksheet: Color me!
Worksheet: Sun, moon, and stars
Bible craft: Make a paper boat
Worksheet: Big and small
Worksheet: What can you taste?
Bible puzzle: What did the angel tell Paul?
Worksheet: A is for angel
Worksheet: Counting practice
Coloring page: God will save everyone
Bible flashcards

 Closing prayer:

End the lesson with a small prayer.

Julius

Julius was a Roman soldier (Acts 27:1). He took Paul to Rome by ship. Trace the word. Color the picture.

Julius

🌿 Color me! 🌿

The storm was bad (Acts 27:14).
The men could not see the sun and stars.
Color the objects that you see in the sky.

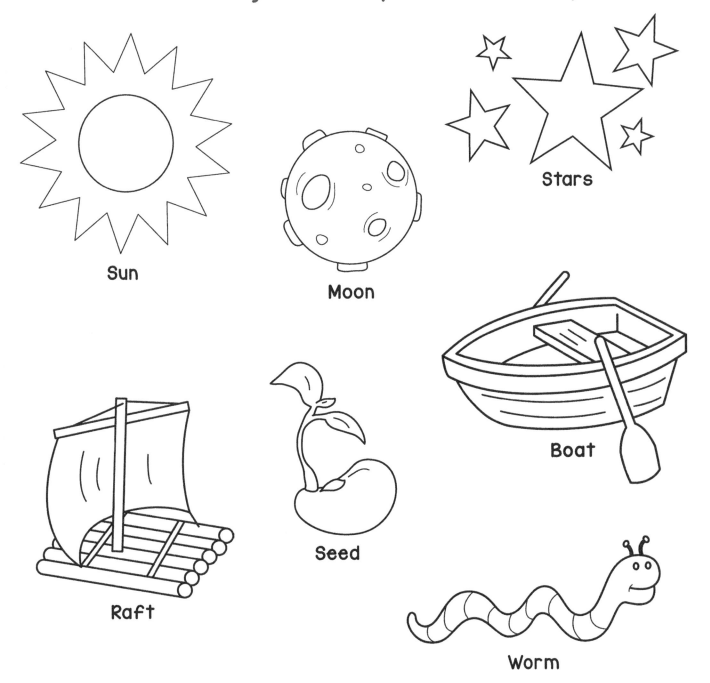

Sun

Moon

Stars

Boat

Raft

Seed

Worm

🌿 Sun Moon Stars 🌿

The men did not see the sun and stars for many days (Acts 27:20). Trace the sun, moon, and star. Color the pictures.

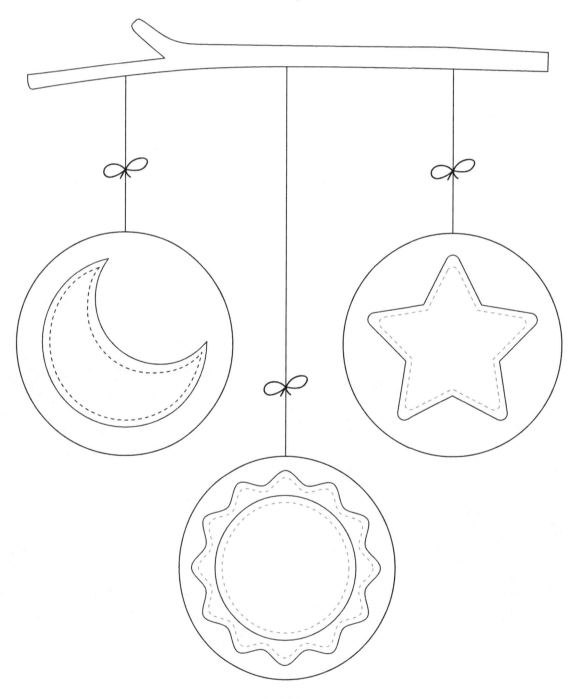

Make a Paper Boat

You will need:
1. Paper plates
2. Paint, felt pens, or crayons
3. Construction or thick paper
4. Scissors (adult only)
5. Extra-strength glue sticks or tape

Instructions:

1. From the construction or thick paper, cut out a square or rectangle in the shape of a boat hull for the hull, a long thin rectangle for the mast, and a triangle for the sail.
2. Have your child draw waves or water onto the bottom of the paper plate. This is the sea the boat will sail on.
3. Glue the boat pieces (boat hull, mast, and sail) together to form a boat.
4. Fold the paper plate in half and glue the boat onto the paper plate's fold.

❧ Big & small ❧

Paul sailed to Rome in a big ship (Acts 27:2).
A sailing ship is big. A rowboat is small.

big

small

Draw something big.   Draw something small.

What can you taste?

The storm was bad. Paul and the men did not eat food for many days (Acts 27:33). Color the items you can taste.

What did the angel tell Paul?

Fill in the blanks using the chart below.

Can you read the sentence?

__ __ __ __ __ __ __
4 15 14 15 20 2 5

__ __ __ __ __ __
1 6 18 1 9 4

A	B	C	D	E	F	G	H	I	J	K	L	M
1	2	3	4	5	6	7	8	9	10	11	12	13

N	O	P	Q	R	S	T	U	V	W	X	Y	Z
14	15	16	17	18	19	20	21	22	23	24	25	26

✹ A is for Angel ✹

is for

Angel

Counting practice

Color the square with the correct number of objects in each box.

"God will save everyone on this ship... "

(Acts 27:24)

LESSON 4 | Lesson Plan
Shipwrecked!

Teacher: _____

Today's Bible passage: Acts 27:27-44

Welcome prayer:
Pray a simple prayer with the children before you begin the lesson.

Lesson objectives:
In this lesson, children will learn:
1. How a group of sailors tried to escape
2. How the men reached the island of Malta

Did You Know?
Paul's Hebrew name was Sha'ul. His Greek name was Paul.

Bible lesson overview:
The sailors were close to an island. They threw anchors into the sea to stop the ship from hitting the rocks. A group of sailors wanted to escape in a small boat. Paul said, "If these men escape, you will all die." So, the soldiers did not let the men go. That morning, Paul said to the men, "Eat some food so you can stay alive." Everyone on the ship ate bread until they were full. Then they threw the grain into the sea to make the ship lighter. When daylight came, the men saw an island. They jumped into the sea and swam to the island. Everyone on the boat was saved. But the big waves broke the ship into pieces.

Let's Review:

Questions to ask your students:

1. How did the men stop the ship hitting the rocks?
2. What did Paul tell everyone on the ship to do?
3. How did Paul and the men get to the island?
4. What happened to the ship?
5. Did God keep His promise to save everyone on the ship?

 A memory verse to help children remember God's Word:

"The sailors saw land." (Acts 27:39)

Activities:

Worksheet: I can count!

Worksheet: A is for anchor

Worksheet: G is for grain

Worksheet: Sacks of grain

Alphabet worksheet: B is for bread

Worksheet: Let's eat!

Worksheet: Fish math

Labyrinth: Help Paul swim to the island of Malta

Coloring page: Shipwrecked!

 Closing prayer:

End the lesson with a small prayer.

❧I can count!❧

What a lot of sea animals.
Count them and write the number in the box.

A is for anchor

An anchor is a heavy object that stops a boat or ship from moving. Trace the words. Color the picture.

a

anchor

A is for anchor

✹ G is for grain ✹

is for

grain

🌿 Sacks of grain 🌿

The men threw sacks of grain into the sea to make the ship lighter (Acts 27:18). Glue popcorn onto the sack to fill it with grain.

B is for Bread

Paul told the men to eat bread (Acts 27:34).
Trace the letters. Color the picture.

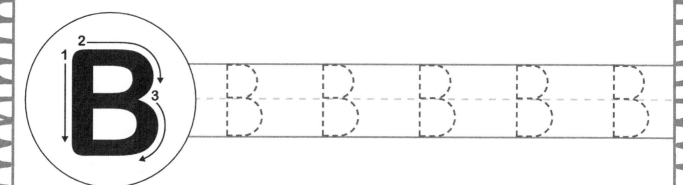

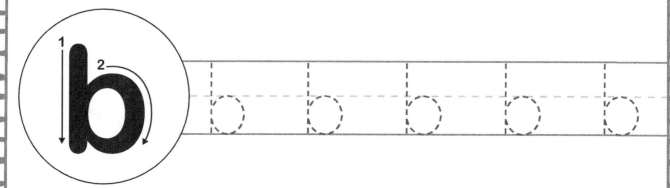

 Trace the letter b

Color the bread

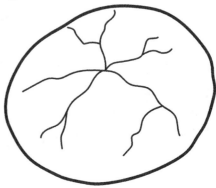

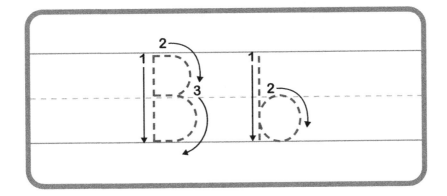

Try writing these letters on your own.

🌿 Let's eat! 🌿

Paul told the men to eat bread so they could stay alive (Acts 27:35-36). Circle and color the words that rhyme with eat.

EAT

beat

seat

meat

clock

❧ Fish math ❧

Roll a dice and color the fish with the same number.

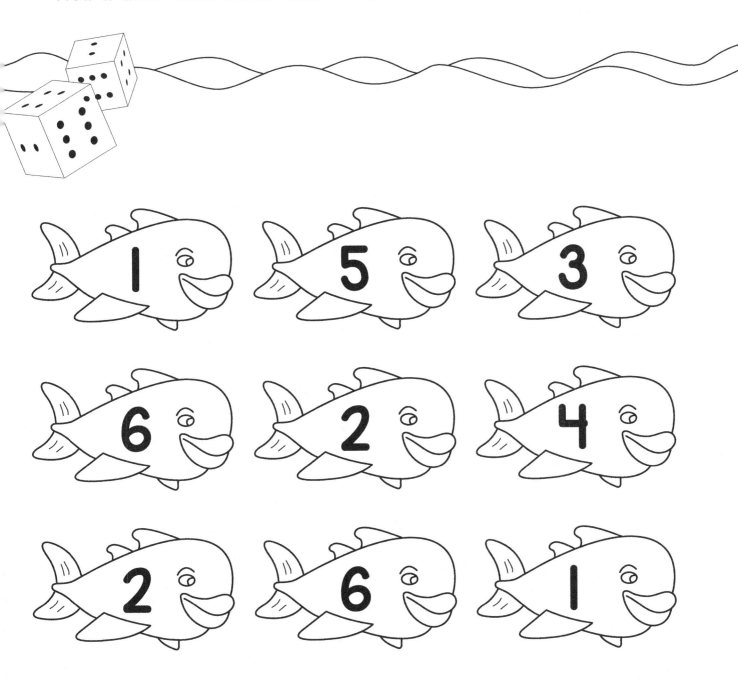

🌿 Shipwrecked! 🌿

Help Paul and Julius swim to the island of Malta.

"The big waves broke the Ship into pieces."

(Acts 27:41)

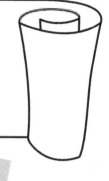

LESSON 5 | Lesson Plan
Paul and the snake

Teacher: _____

Today's Bible passage: Acts 28:1-11

Welcome prayer:
Pray a simple prayer with the children before you begin the lesson.

Lesson objectives:
In this lesson, children will learn:
1. How Paul was bitten by a snake
2. How long Paul and the men were shipwrecked on Malta

Did You Know?
Paul was shipwrecked on an island called Malta.

Bible lesson overview:
After Paul and the men arrived on the island of Malta, the local people were kind. They built a fire so everyone could stay warm. While Paul stood by the fire, he was bitten by a snake. But he shook off the snake into the fire and was not hurt. The local people were surprised. "This man must be a god!" they said. Paul stayed on the island for three months. There, he prayed and healed many sick people. After three months, the ship's captain was ready to leave Malta and sail to Rome. It was time for Paul to meet the Roman emperor!

Let's Review:

Questions to ask your students:

1. How did the people take care of Paul and the men?
2. What bit Paul by the fire?
3. What did Paul do to the snake?
4. How long did Paul stay on the island of Malta?
5. Why did Paul sail to Italy?

 A memory verse to help children remember God's Word:

"Paul was not hurt." (Acts 28:5)

Activities:

Coloring page: Island of Malta
Bible word search puzzle: Shipwrecked!
Worksheet: Paul on Malta
Worksheet: Trace the words
Worksheet: Bitten by a snake!
Worksheet: Paul on Malta
Coloring page: Paul and the snake
Worksheet: Hot & cold
Bible craft: Bitten by a snake!
Worksheet: The number three
Tracing activity: Help Paul get to Rome
Worksheet: What's different?
Worksheet: Match the pictures
Worksheet: Let's draw
Worksheet: True or false?
Certificate of award

 Closing prayer:

End the lesson with a small prayer.

"...the island was called Malta."

(Acts 28:1)

🌿 Shipwrecked! 🌿

Find and circle each of the words from the list below.

```
P A U L W S
H P T I A N
M E N Q R A
J O B W M K
S H I P O E
F I R E Z Z
```

SNAKE   PAUL
FIRE   MEN
SHIP   WAVE

🌿 Paul on Malta 🌿

Paul was bitten by a snake. He was not hurt (Acts 28:5).
Trace the word snake. Circle and color the
pictures that start with the letter s.

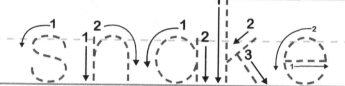

socks

scarf

snake

coin

Trace the Words

Color the pictures.

pray

fire

sea

snake

🍃 Bitten by a snake! 🍃

A snake came out of the fire and bit Paul's hand.
But the snake did not hurt him (Acts 28:5).
Use the color code to finish the picture.

| 1 = green | 2 = red | 3 = yellow | 4 = brown |

Paul on Malta

The people on Malta were kind. They made a fire so everyone was warm. Paul and the men were happy (Acts 28:2). Trace the words. Color the pictures.

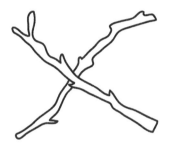

Paul put sticks on the fire

The fire was hot

The men were happy

"Paul shook the snake into the fire and was not hurt."

(Acts 28:5)

🌿 Hot & cold 🌿

On Malta, it was raining and cold (Acts 28:2).
The people built a fire so Paul could get warm.
Water is cold. A fire is hot.

hot

cold

Draw something hot.

Draw something cold.

✦ The number three ✦

Paul stayed on the island for three months.
Write the number 3. Color the pictures.

❧ Help Paul get to Rome ❧

Help Paul sail to Rome by tracing along the line.

What's different?

Circle the picture that is different.

❧ Match the pictures ❧

Read the sentence. Draw a line to the picture it matches with.

1. I see a ship.

2. I see an anchor.

3. I see fire.

4. I see a snake.

anchor

ship

snake

fire

🌿 Let's Draw 🌿

Draw Paul shipwrecked on the island of Malta.
Use your imagination!

❧ True or False? ❧

Listen to the statements. Are they true or false?

Paul flew to Rome.	Julius was a teacher.
An angel spoke to Paul.	Paul swam to the island.
Paul was eaten by a snake.	The storm was very bad.

CRAFTS & PROJECTS

❧ Paul in prison ❧

1. Color the picture of Paul. Cut out the box.
2. Punch a hole in the dots at the top and bottom of the page.
3. Weave string or pipe cleaners through the matching top and bottom holes to create a prison cell.

Paul sails to Rome

Color and cut out the people. Glue them onto the ship.

soldier   Paul   captain

🌿 My compass 🌿

A strong wind blew from the south (Acts 27:13).
Which direction is south? Trace the letters
on the compass. Cut out the words and place
them next to the correct direction.

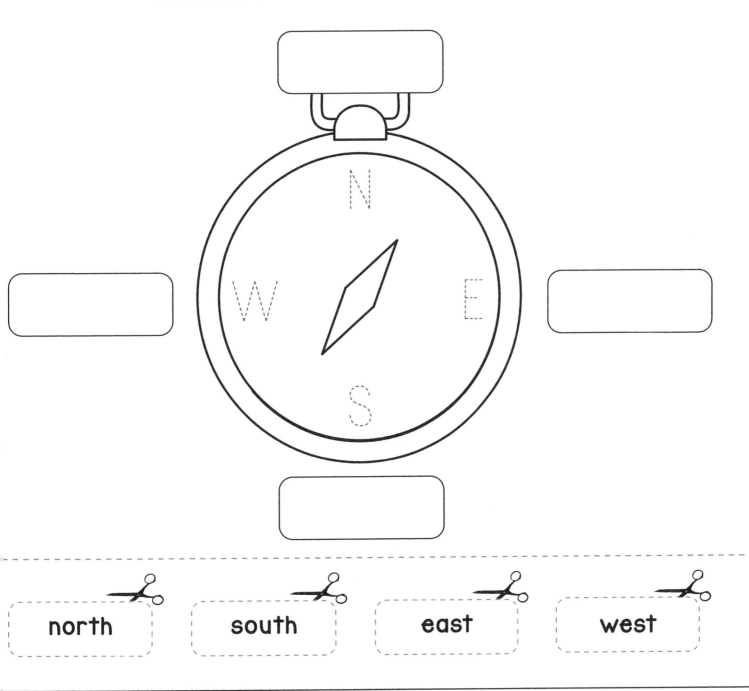

✂ north ✂ south ✂ east ✂ west

Flashcards

Color and cut out the flashcards.
Tape them around your house or classroom!

Rome

5

wind

6

Julius

7

anchor

8

🌿 Bitten by a snake! 🌿

Color and cut out the pictures. Paste them onto the island.

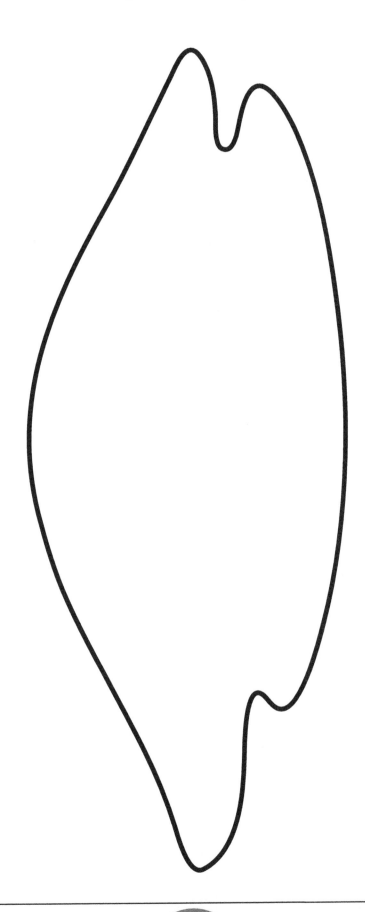

Certificate of Award

Certificate of Award

Congratulations

....

For

....

....
Signed

ANSWER KEY

LESSON ONE: Paul sails to Rome
Let's Review answers:
1. The religious leaders did not like Paul telling people about the Messiah
2. The Romans
3. The Roman emperor
4. Julius
5. Paul traveled to Rome by ship

LESSON TWO: Paul's Warning
Let's review answers:
1. Because it was windy
2. It is better to stay in Fair Havens until the weather improves
3. No
4. There was a safe harbor in Phoenix
5. Prompt children to tell you what they have learned about Paul

LESSON THREE: The Storm
Let's review answers:
1. They threw the boat's cargo overboard
2. The storm was bad
3. God will save everyone on the ship, but the ship will be destroyed
4. The sun or the stars
5. No – Paul had faith in God

LESSON FOUR: Shipwrecked!
Let's review answers:
1. They threw the boat's anchors into the sea
2. Eat bread
3. Paul and the men swam to the island
4. The ship was destroyed by the sea
5. Yes, God kept His promise to save everyone on the ship

LESSON FIVE: Paul and the snake
Let's review answers:
1. They built a fire
2. A poisonous snake
3. He shook off the snake into the fire
4. Three months
5. To meet the Roman Emperor

True or False?
Answers:
Paul flew to Rome. (False)
Julius was a teacher. (False)
An angel spoke to Paul. (True)
Paul swam to the island. (True)
Paul was eaten by a snake. (False)
The storm was very bad. (True)

Discover more Activity Books!

Available for purchase at www.biblepathwayadventures.com

INSTANT DOWNLOAD!

Paul's Shipwreck (Beginners)
The Fall Feasts
Paul's Journeys
Noah's Ark (Beginners)
Moses Ten Plagues (Beginners)
Moses Ten Plagues
Paul's Shipwreck
Twelve Tribes of Israel (Beginners)

Made in the USA
Monee, IL
08 September 2023

42377465R00052